"RELOCATION"
AND OTHER POEMS

By

r. y. takagi

For bird,
thank you for
helping me learn to
fly !

love,
[signature]

ACKNOWLEDGMENTS

This book, in this form, exists thanks to the talents and generous spirit of one Alex M. Frankel. Nominated to be in the *Best New Poets of 2013* volume by Judith Hall and essayist extraordinaire, Frankel is the founder and host of the monthly Second Sunday Poetry Series which takes place at the Studio Theatre at St. Denis Building (Los Angeles Historic-Cultural Monument #763).

The Studio Theatre was the former home and work space of Ruth St. Denis, America's Mother of Modern Dance, and is now the home base for the Valentina Oumansky Dramatic Dance Foundation. Through Frankel's work with the foundation's president, Tarumi Takagi-Inouye, this collection serves as a legacy for the Takagi Family.

We would also like to thank r. y. takagi's siblings, and dear family friend and artist Shinkichi Tajiri. Hopefully, the indignities they, and many other Americans of Japanese descent, suffered while interned during World War II find new meaning thanks to r. y. takagi's creative expression through haiku.

ISBN-13: 978-1493551842
ISBN-10: 1493551841

Cover art/Drawing: Conte drawing on paper, 1942, by Shinkichi Tajiri (1923 Los Angeles, Ca. - 2009 Baarlo, The Netherlands) while interned at Poston III. Tajiri was a veteran of the 442nd Regimental Combat Team, a renowned sculptor, photographer and filmmaker. He moved to and studied in Paris on a GI bill in 1946. Lived and worked in the Netherlands from 1956 until his passing. We are grateful to Giotta Tajiri for giving permission to use this artwork.

Photos: All photographs are from Takagi Family albums – see p. 66 for descriptions.

To Jacqueline and Sara

CONTENTS

FOREWORD

I graduated from the Pasadena Playhouse in 1951 and spent the following summer working in an aircraft factory in San Diego, California where I met Bob Takagi, who remained a close friend forever after. That fall I moved to Hollywood and began to study with an important acting coach, Helen Freeman, and it was she who introduced Bob and me to Nyogen Senzaki, a Buddhist priest, who held services in his Zendo in the Miyako Hotel in Los Angeles. It was there that we learned about the haiku. Senzaki-san was a fully realized man, the first I had ever encountered, who lived fully in present-time, and the atmosphere he created lent itself to writing a haiku that was an original. This spoke to Bob in particular and the haiku became his way of expressing his inner truth.

Ken Chapin

"RELOCATION"

U.S. CITIZEN
(CIRCA 1942)

no no not for you
you go to internment camp
you non-alien*

---

* non-alien: a term devised and used in 1942 to denote American citizens of
Japanese ancestry.

DEFINITIONS

Imperial Japan bombed Pearl Harbor on December 7, 1941. Then the U.S. entered World War II on the side of Britain and France against Germany, Italy, and Japan. All Japanese-Americans were considered possible spies and sympathizers.

Relocation   The ordered eviction and guarded transporting, to a place of confinement, of a specific group of people: those of Japanese descent, citizens and "non-citizens" (or as some officials would have it, aliens and "non-aliens") for the purpose of "internment" in places to be known as Relocation Centers. (Legal, oriental non-citizens were denied naturalization by laws dating back to the exclusion act of 1882.)
[Previous to this date only free whites could be naturalized, and after the Civil War, citizenship was extended to black people and their descendants.]

Assembly Center   An existing location, such as race tracks, fairgrounds, etc. where a large, specific group of "evacuees" could be confined, by fenced enclosure and guarded by military personnel, while awaiting transfer to a more permanent "Relocation Center."

Relocation Center   Hastily built "internment" camps in remote areas to confine approximately 118 thousand people deemed dangerous to *their* country, and removed from their homes and properties which existed within a delineated, "exclusionary area." Said camps, or centers, were enclosed by fences and "protected" by guard towers manned by military personnel.

"RELOCATION CENTER"

I still wonder how
they had processed such a name
for this lousy place

12

EVACUATION
(CIRCA 1942)

EXECUTIVE ORDER 9066[†]

there it was again
tacked on the telephone pole
in case we missed it

CONTRABAND

brownie camera
smashed and buried in the ground
with anger and tears

LUGGAGE

"you may take with you
only what you can carry"
and then—that was it

THE HOWLING

it came: gust of wind,
uprooting, devastating,
and then—we were gone

"ALL ABOARD"

riding in the train
with the strict ordered closed blinds
by soldiers with guns

[†] On February 2, 1942 President F. D. Roosevelt signed Executive Order 9066, sending Japanese-Americans to internment camps.

ASSEMBLY CENTER

THE ARRIVAL

people old and young
spilling out of the train cars
then tagged like items

FAMILY QUARTERS

that famous race horse
we are sleeping in his stall
all seven of us

HE KNEW

what is that strange scent
coming from the whitewashed walls?
"son, that is horse piss"

GENERATIONS
(THREE CUTS OF A SWORD)

again up the hill
under weight against the wind
and the gods laughing

a cruel cut was made
just before the budding time
what now the season

yesterday is lost
tomorrow is of wishing
today is "in camp"

AUGUST 1942

Relocation to Poston, Arizona, under military guard. The three camps that comprised Poston became the third largest community in Arizona.

RELOCATION

En Route

blinded train windows
east through the desert morning
sound of not knowing

Out There

loud incessant roar
armored tanks desert training
slanted eyes peeking

Parker, Arizona

off the dusty train
onto designated bus
Poston here we come

Flat Miles

over new gravel
desert hot and foreboding
road to internment

Arrival

block 329
in Poston Camp # III
—JAP RELOCATED—

POSTON

looking past the fence
and standing on your tip toes
you could see Nowhere

STORM

sand and blinding dust
the stinging wind hard and coarse
dry and foul tasting

BEQUEATH

WHY

when the fire came
the trees, they did not resist
and they did not run

KICKED

hey, it was my ass
look to your own to suffer
it will come in time

~

MONDAY '41

oh how rude it was
that slamming of the door
on December eighth

CHRONICLE

SPRING

sudden gust of wind
startles a young plum blossom
will it will it not

SONG

why that way flowing
and off the broad leaves falling
dew into a fugue

WHY

I was ordered there
I was removed and put there
there is a why there

~

HYPHENATED-AMERICAN

1942

I did not know it
that I was hyphenated
till I was interned

TWO-SIDED GLASS

would you tell me please
what is your hyphenation
pale colored man

~

CHILDREN OF THE SUN

And

HAIKU BETWEEN THE WINDS

BEYOND THE FENCE
(POSTON INTERNMENT CAMP III, 1942)

Black Mountain is there
alone on the horizon
where the sun rises

between the mountain
and a water tank tower
a day moon looks down

a desert here where
footsteps follow no others
and absent are dreams

beyond no counting
some shade under a smoke tree
a listening place

across the abyss
out of the day moon's shadow
a coyote howls

rising from the sand
is a time place beginning
blown there by a wind

in that desert wash
footprints backwards in the sand
to water tank tower

EPILOGUE

from the folds of time
echoes as old coyote
howls at a day moon

SHELL TOWN

DREAM

Shell Town by the Sea
stillborn Depression baby
willy-nilly blown

SMALL WORLD

Shell Town at Main Street
beyond are other places
there is one bus stop

ON MAIN STREET

a grocery store
and the Shell Town Auto Court
and a gas station

SUMMER NIGHTS

bench seated singers
on Sunday go to meeting
loud through open door

PROMISE

Una street went south
past open fields to the bay
there was nothing there

FILBERT STREET

there was Filbert street
a dirt road with concrete curbs
others had no curbs

GUAVA STREET

a stretch of dirt road
with seven scattered houses
the green one was ours

RESIDENTS

skin of Mexico
Africa Japan and Sweden
and some other whites

OLD MAN BUTTON

his house just sat there
in the middle of a pond
every time it rained

YONDER

an old wooden barn
a landmark off to the east
hard red in the sun

ON THE HILL

on up the dirt road
a yellow house stands alone
no one lives there now

ABANDONED . . .

old broken shack
standing there among weeds
unable to speak

. . . AND MUTE

sunlight through the cracks
and dried crap in a corner
doors and windows gone

TRACKS

intruder to the fields
between Shell Town and the bay
hard rails for commerce

BRIDGE

a bridge on Main Street
west of where the memories are
that's all that remains

END

Shell Town Is No More
it did not change it is gone
the dream just went broke

~

CHESS

I was very young
and Mr. Trowbridge was old
and we would play chess

I stared at the board
quite sure of my decision
I removed my hand

"Are you sure you want that move?"
and sure enough, I did not

REMEMBER

"Dibs I saw it first"
shiny penny on the ground
then a candy smile

SALZBURG

yesterday recedes
into the hills to decay
archbishop driven

there the sound of dead armies
half hidden among the trees

SHARING

did you see it there
in the sky a falling star
"huh, a falling star?"

THAT HOUSE

why did they paint it
pink on the outside and not
pink on the inside

PA

"What are you digging?"
"A fence post hole, want to help?"
"No, it's too much work"

"Too bad, there's so much to learn
in the making of a hole"

GUEST

you do not know me
yet you eat my strawberries
snail you are a thief

OLD ELM

your leaves are so small
will you make shade this summer
newly pruned elm tree

WIND TAKEN

a dewed leaf falls
and the grass below accepts
did anyone hear

KNELL

he rubbed his eyebrow
for he could not remember
how he had grown old

INFLATION

three cent postage stamp
now you are thirty-seven
my how you have grown

CHRISTMAS OF 1941

dirty sneaky Jap
he said to the Chinese boy
they all look alike

AMINO ACID

did I hear a lamb
in a bulb it came to be
from a red brown soup

hydrogen methane water
heated and then lightning struck

ATTENZIONE

little pebble thrown
against a window sounding
crickets singing stop

BELL TOWER

did the bell hear it
as it passed so gently by
the donkey's farting

A CONVERSATION WITH ERNEST HEMINGWAY
by r. y. takagi (pvt. US ARMY)

Cortina, Italy. 1948.

> he poured chianti
> and we just began to talk
> I was twenty-one

EH: Were you put in one of those camps? ("relocation center" U.S.A.)
ryt: Yes.
EH: How do you feel about it?
ryt: It was a shitty deal. But what can you do except chalk it up to experience?
EH: Everyone gets kicked in the head sometime in life. You're lucky that you learned early. Some never do.

> all that we have is
> experiences that's it
> there are five of them

what you do and what happens to you; friends; family; someone you love; and if you're religious—religion.

and Hemingway talked on:

> AS A BOY

> potatoes planted
> around the stumps of cut trees
> they did it that way

AS A YOUNG MAN

night driving flat miles
windshield wiper sloshing
on to Mexico

WWII
(in the apple orchards)

each and every day
I needed forty minutes
just to be alone

I would throw apples
at those who would disturb me
in my perch above

TOMORROW

what science will bring
all the possibilities
harnessing the sun

~

*it was his laughter
that I remember mostly
it included me*

~

PEPPER AND ISOLT

often it visits
is there a name for it then
your pain beyond pain

PROGRESS

he climbed down the tree
and then invented the saw
then cut down the tree

THE COPPER KETTLE

MORNING

there where the curb ends
in the splat of last night's puke
a pair of false teeth

NIGHT

alone with this song
bumping on with the street lamps
the door closed behind

NEED

he kept on looking
for that something he needed
in the wrong places

END

there was no singing
for Time had broken his glass
and Saki moved on

~

THE OLD SINGER

OLD SONG

listen to the rhythms
foot driven machine stitch singing
song of shirt making

OLD DANCE

thrust through pull to taut
return of point eye intent
thread and cloth dance on

OLD SINGER

sunlight slanting through
soft curtains to the Singer
by an empty chair

~

A HAND-ME-DOWN

ONCE UPON A

in San Diego
crossing a street long ago
a man and a boy

QUESTION

the signal turned green
and they stepped off of the curb
"what makes you happy?"

LONG STEP

step in suspension
with the sunlight and the stars
then the sound of step down

ANSWER

"a sense of being
when it is experienced"
and they crossed the street

~

SENZAKI NYOGEN
(A HOMELESS ZEN MONK)

FESTIVAL

the parade passed by
"what did you like the best Sensei?"
"the young dancing girls"

SERMON

he held up a rose
and found one smile in the group
he gave it the rose

SHE ASKED

how he dealt with sex
he ushered her to the door
and then shut her out

ACCIDENT

it fell to the floor
and I stared as it transformed
beauty into pieces

after echoes I looked up
he stood there with broom in hand

TEA WITH FRIENDS

"tea ceremony"
"such exquisite artistry"
"pure grace in movement"

Senzaki took up his cup
and drank his tea then smiled

~

MR. TAMALA

THE 1930S

pulling his old cart
searching endlessly through trash
for something to sell

TEA TIME

in a blackened can
he brewed his lemon leaf tea
and shared it with me

SABBATH WINE

old Tamala slept
sprawled under the pepper tree
a smile on his face

~

STOLEN BASES

To Do

a neighborhood street
or an empty lot would do
just a little space

Make Do

and then we shaped it
with whatever we could find
we made a diamond

Also

any kind of ball
and a good stick for batting
and we were ready

Election

the best players were
chosen to be the captains
we knew who they were

The Toss

a toss of the bat
then hand over hand to top
oh no no cappies

SIDES

win the toss pick first
captains assign positions
odd man umpires

EXEMPTION

own a real bat
or a genuine baseball
yes you get to play

FIRST UP

toss for first to bat
we play according to rules
and we make the rules

IN THE SUN

we played in the sun
the trees grew and the grass grew
and yes so did we

~

XANADU WEST: PHEASANT HUNT
(FOR ANITA AND HERMAN)

someone had decreed
that a place like this should be
it was that guy Khan

the dust settled down
and the desert hills were ours
and we accepted

sun chased shadows gone
the air crisp and sinus clear
this then was a day

and we unwrapped it
with crackling expectation
and hard-boiled eggs

and pepper and salt
tomatoes and cucumbers
and hot rich coffee

uncapped effusion
into the desert morning
for this was our dome

across the valley
where no man has ever walked
huge red shapes of rock

and below a train
passing on its destined way
saying its hello

and here on the ground
little creatures scurrying
into their caverns

in meditation
cross-legged on a carpet
Kublai saw and heard

meditate a dot
isolate a breath and squeeze
and the mountains roar

sounds of paradise
and the taste of honey-dew
with the sky ringing

and echoes again
and again down the river
to that sunless sea

the sun was going
and so perforce was our day
we sipped our cognac

and we were happy
and Kublai was happy too
and we sipped again

BEYOND THE FIELDS

NORTHWEST

a raw wooden fence
encircles the tract houses
stopping them for now

WEST

on the horizon
no more clean line of the hill
only rooftops now

SOUTH

"for sale six acres
future commercial zoning"
a sign in the field

~

WALKING
(NEAR INOUYE FARM)

morning on the road
with fresh scent of plowed fields
and birds descending

a rusted old nail
and a run-over beer can
here at side of road

along an old road
wires strung to tall brown poles
talking to the wind

the night sky arrives
slow turning to purple shades
the birds are leaving

MR. BURKE

scratching and pecking
of a sudden he was there
in the yard in March

where had he come from
so majestic yet alone
red wattle and crown

when he first saw me
he crackled bur-ur-ur-ke
so I called him Burke

he took the thrown bread
then came closer and looked up
took bread from my hand

then came banana lunch
he pecked and it was soon gone
most of the peel too

waking from my nap
I looked out through the window
there was Burke napping

a few days later
as shadows were lengthening
I happened outside

seeing me Burke stopped
he started back from the road
but I was busy

when I looked again
the quiet road was empty
Mr. Burke had gone

he had left behind
a little tuft of feather
waiting for the wind

the sun was setting
and the night came quietly
Mr. Burke was gone

after sunset memories
a feather floats on the wind

SUNRISE CAFÉ
(OCTOBER BREAKFAST)

biscuits and gravy
overwhelming a large plate
the house specialty

decorated walls
homey hobby crafted themes
to make grandma smile

out of the kitchen
loud over breakfast tables
chatter of caged birds

old vinyl booth seats
sink to board as they deflate
knees and elbows rise

waitresses moving
like pool balls on a table
as they walk the walk

denim and nylon
wearing caps that advertise
waiting for hot cakes

with summer's fullness
faces that don't ask questions
smile at the hash brown

October pumpkins
waddle in obese and round
seek empty tables

legs like jugglers move
round and large through the doorway
one by one they go

now in from the cold
mama and two baby bears
scent of honey here

did I hear oatmeal
small orange juice and coffee
and hold the butter

JOE AND MARCH WIND

BOAT

a little toy boat
set adrift on the water
now finds a current

FLOATING

soap bubble floating
iridescent on a wind
swoops upward and Pop

SPRING

there are peach blossoms
on the branches of my tree
wind takes one away

SOTTO VOCE

something engaging
smiling in his quiet song
soft to cadence end

DOORS

through the open door
came singing from over there
and scent of new leaves

~

ASSISTED LIVING

in the dining room
tink of fork and sip of spoon
voices hunched and grey

MR. MORROW

God damn it Morrow
that our paths should cross should cross
and they did they did

HOW OLD

looking out and in
there at the open window
I sit and wonder

it was fifty years ago
and again just yesterday

FOUR!!!!

they have all teed off
and gone down the last fairway
where the sun goes down

they are all gone now
to that place where shadows go
when the sun goes down

all gone down the last fairway
Hal, Steve, Jerry, and Byron

DIES IRAE

the Monterey pines
sap bleeding they are dying
rusting in the wind

ZERO

and where did it go
after one and god and all
that little zero

S. E. AND ALZHEIMER

MOVING

beyond the shadows
is there sunlight on the road
any sun at all

FLOWING

is the light bending
or fracturing as it goes
crashing into leaves

SINGING

the wind blows gently
the wisps of remaining clouds
into the echoes

~

GOODBYE TO‡

ALAN

he leaves his luggage
and walks beyond the oak trees
into the sunshine

HELEN

her laughter is there
colors in the herb garden
shade among the oaks

AND BEATO

the almond tree and
the night fireflies were there
and the wind was still

her hands had held the whirl
of songs that gathered us in

~

‡ The Ranch House—Ojai, California

HARUE[§]

hands unhurried move
deliberate with the day
having found the Art

HARUE

inside listening
to the songs her children sang
she hummed quietly

CHRYSANTHEMUM

"hey Pop, a flower!
I thought they bloomed in the fall"
"it made a mistake"

[§]r. y. takagi's mother

FLIGHT 5-7-9

WAITING

Sara** in April
she runs and jumps with laughter
splashes in a rain

IN FLIGHT

in flight high high up
just one month "five years old"
and Kogoro†† smiles

CELEBRATE (MAY 7TH)

how old are you now
she raises five fingers up
"I am five years old"

BUT

"my face feels like four
but in back my head says five"
on this day in May

~

JACQI[‡‡]
(WHEN SHE WAS THREE)

Jaca-r-r-r-randa tree
I have learned to roll my r's
my mama taught me

PREDICATE

"to possess or hold
the advance of beauty" is
TARUMI[§§]—your name

they say it means "much beauty"
but Grand Pa was different

VLO[***]

she ran with the wind
opening doors with laughter
letting in the sun

[‡‡]r. y. takagi's older granddaughter
[§§]r. y. takagi's daughter
[***]r. y. takagi's wife, Valentina Lubova Oumansky

57

PLEASE

tell me a story
that is yours not collected
bibliography

CHESS MOVE

I saw three choices
and selected the best one
so why did I lose

IRON WOOD

sliding in the curves
beyond the straight edge of time
to a moment found

cactus fracturing sunlight
into this desert morning

CHARACTERS

youth's dreams in the wind
tumbling on with other things
into a music

PRETTY

sand without footprints
no path into the forest
but leaves are falling

BIRDS

I watch the robins
in their labor through the day
because I am old!

DOG TROT

stray dogs slow trotting
down the alleyways sniffing
to an endless tune

R. E. PETTIS

"that son of a bitch!
did you see him cut me off?
he drives just like me"

NOVEMBER

the road is still there
but the winds are gentle now
shall I flip a coin?

SPECTACLES

astigmatic moon
when I first saw two of you
I thought I was drunk

HOWDY

from the yin of night
comes the slow advance of day
and good yang to you

RETRO

a lone white towel
pinned hanging from a clothes line
by a wooden pin

WITH ME

an old stone lantern
and chrysanthemums in bloom
warming in the sun

MAS AND RINA

BIRCH

first light and the sun
quiver dancing with birch leaves
all dressed up in gold

ELM

the grand old elm tree
standing huge beside the sun
bowing to a wind

~

MY GRANDDAUGHTERS

A RECITAL

Jacqi bowed then played
and I smiled all the while to
the music she made

SARA

into her small hands
I placed a sweet green apple
and she said "thank you"

~

PALE YELLOW HOUSE
(CIRCA 1935)

it stood there alone
at the west end of the road
a house on a hill

it was just a house
but it seemed tall standing there
alone in the sun

the dirt road wandered
past the house and disappeared
just beyond the rise

it had been said that
people had lived there before
the windows went blank

no clouds passed it by
no one there about the house
only vacant sky

and it was yellow
that house alone on the hill
it was pale yellow

HEARTBURN

like a burp they come
those undigested numbers
nine zero six six

FLAME

O when we were young
the joy and the pain of it
good for a lifetime

PHOTO DESCRIPTIONS

Page 11: c. 1942 - r. y. takagi around the age he was interned in camp and taken by camp photographer Paul Shintaku.

Page 15: September, 1954 - r. y. takagi inside 329-6-B, Poston III, AZ with his "rediscovered toy." Nearly a decade after leaving camp, r. y. takagi and friend Raymond Fuller (photographer), drove through Arizona and stopped to see what was left of Poston III. The only block of barracks still standing was Block 329, his family's former abode; all the others had been torn down. There, left behind as if some kind of beacon, he found a toy his father designed and eldest brother, Fudo Takagi, made. Decades later, Fudo made a beautiful display box for the artifact and donated it to the Japanese American Historical Society of San Diego.

Page 19: c. 1922 - Harue Takagi holding Fudo Takagi, r. y. takagi's mother and eldest brother – From Takagi Family album, likely taken by Kogoro Takagi or Ben Yamamoto (Harue's brother).

Page 33: 1948 – Ernest Hemingway, Robert Pepper, and r. y. takagi while stationed in Italy.

Page 43: c. 1950s – r. y. takagi enjoying his favorite pastimes, hunting and fishing.

Page 57: c. 1960s – r. y. takagi and wife, Valentina Oumansky

Page 61: c. 1948 – r. y. takagi while stationed in Italy, where he developed his astigmatism.

Page 65: 1960 Japan – r. y. takagi and wife, Valentina Oumansky, during his only trip to the land of his ancestors.

Page 67: March, 2007 – Taken at The Ranch House in Ojai, CA. Valentina Oumansky, Jacqueline Mika Inouye, Karl Inouye, r. y. takagi, Sara Aiko Inouye, & Tarumi Alina Takagi-Inouye

ABOUT THE AUTHOR

Robert Yasuo Takagi (1928-2010) was born in San Diego, California, the fourth of five children. During World War II, he and his family were "relocated" and interned in Poston, Arizona. Following his older brothers' bold move, he left camp (which was allowed only if one moved away from the west coast) and went to Chicago. A short time later he joined the army.

While was stationed in Italy, Ernest Hemingway befriended r. y. takagi; this reinforced in him a passion for literature that had been sparked by their mutual army friend Robert Pepper. After his military service, r. y. takagi returned to Chicago. He studied music and art and even sang in a chorus with the Chicago Symphony under the direction of Leonard Bernstein. r. y. takagi moved back to California and in 1955 married dancer and choreographer Valentina Oumansky, with whom he had one daughter, Tarumi.

r. y. takagi spent years editing news and film, and his career as a music editor in the motion picture industry spanned over four decades, with a list of credits that include popular TV series like *Hawaii 5-0, Gunsmoke*, and *The Twilight Zone*. In the last twenty-five years of his life he went back to a passion of his youth, writing haiku poems. This had interested him since a life-changing meeting with Nyogen Senzaki, a Buddhist monk, back in the 1950s. r. y. takagi had an uncanny sense of humor; enjoyed golfing, hunting, and fishing; and he especially loved contemplating on his porch in solitude, stogy in his mouth, composing poetry.

Made in the USA
Middletown, DE
23 December 2021